Simple Solution

Fitting Tack

By Toni McAllister
Illustrations by Jean Abernethy

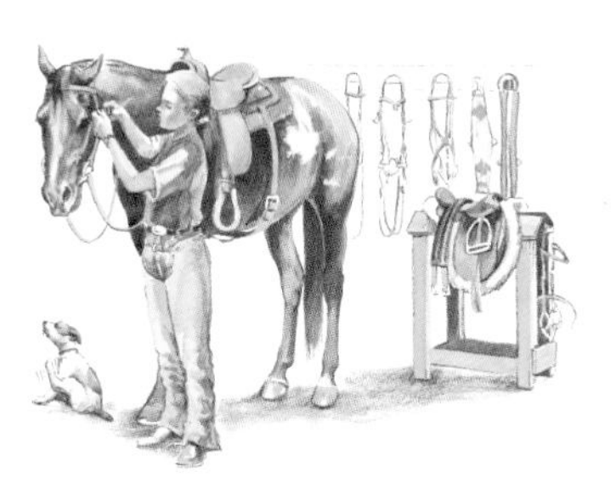

BOWTIE
PRESS®

A Division of BowTie, Inc.
Irvine, California

Dedication

To Winston and Annie—both have taught me well.

The horses in this book are referred to as *she* and *he* in alternating chapters unless their sexes are apparent from the activities discussed.

McAllister, Toni.
Fitting tack / by Toni McAllister ; illustrations by Jean Abernethy.
p. cm. — (Horse illustrated simple solutions)
ISBN-13: 978-1-931993-96-8
ISBN-10: 1-931993-96-3
1. Horsemanship—Equipment and supplies. 2. Horses—Equipment and supplies. I. Title.

SF309.9.M376 2007
636.1'0837—dc22

2006038891

BowTie Press®
A Division of BowTie, Inc.
3 Burroughs
Irvine, California 92618

Printed and bound in Singapore
16 15 14 13 12 11 10 09 08 07   1 2 3 4 5 6 7 8 9 10

CONTENTS

Riding Tack: Fit for You and Your Horse

Imagine taking a weekend hike wearing boots three sizes too big, a small hat that squeezes your head, and a backpack that rubs uncomfortably. Now picture yourself one hour into that hike. How do you think you might feel? Pretty miserable? These discomforts are what our horses endure when they are expected to work in ill-fitting tack.

Aside from giving your horse discomfort, ill-fitting tack is downright dangerous for *both* of you. You don't want to be going down the trail on a saddle that slips out of position—you're likely to fall off, and your horse will probably run loose down the road

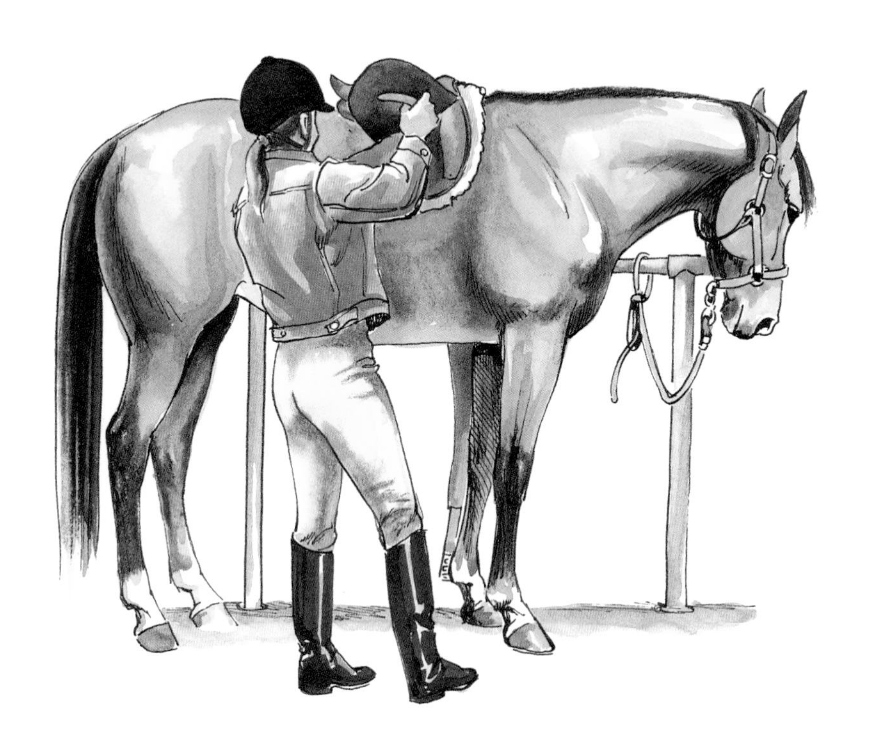

with a saddle under her belly! There's no point in tacking up when the tack isn't functional.

Tack also has to fit the rider. If you fuss and fidget, struggling to get comfortable in a saddle that's either too big or too small for you, it worries your horse. For a mount to feel confident with a rider on her back, the rider must be balanced—nearly impossible in a saddle that's wrong for you! If you're hindered by poor tack fit, your riding skills won't improve, and your time in the saddle will be less enjoyable.

Obtaining equipment that fits properly is the first step toward successful riding, although evaluating fit should be an ongoing process throughout your horse's lifetime. Like people, horses change physically as they age. They lose and gain weight, and their musculature changes as their exercise level varies. Consequently, a saddle that fits your horse today may become a torture device for her in later years. (Imagine squeezing into a pair of jeans from your youth, and you'll get the picture!) Every time you tack up your horse, you should be checking for fit.

When your horse is outfitted in properly fitted tack and you're comfortable in the "driver's seat," riding is more fun—for both of you.

Recognizing When Tack Doesn't Fit Your Horse

A well-trained, healthy horse should accept the tack willingly. If you've ever met a "sour" horse that objected to being tacked up, there's a good chance his equipment didn't fit properly. A horse's resistance to being tacked up and his biting or kicking out when the cinch or the girth is tightened are two signs of fit problems.

If tack-fit problems exist, they only get worse during a ride. Unfortunately, a horse's irritability caused by poorly fitting tack is sometimes interpreted as bad behavior. The rider thinks, "The horse is acting up." In reality, the horse is just trying to communicate that he's in pain. "Ouch, that really hurts!" isn't in his vocabulary.

Good riders investigate the cause of unwanted behaviors in their horses and look for appropriate solutions. They know that any ill-fitting equipment needs to be replaced or adjusted right away, before it causes long-term health or behavioral problems in their horses.

If your horse demonstrates any of the following behaviors while being ridden, he may be trying to tell you he needs some tack attention:

- running off
- rearing
- bucking
- kicking out
- inverting neck and hollowing back
- tossing head
- refusing to accept the bit
- pinning the ears

Not every horse will tell you when something doesn't fit. Unfortunately, some stoic mounts carry on without complaint.

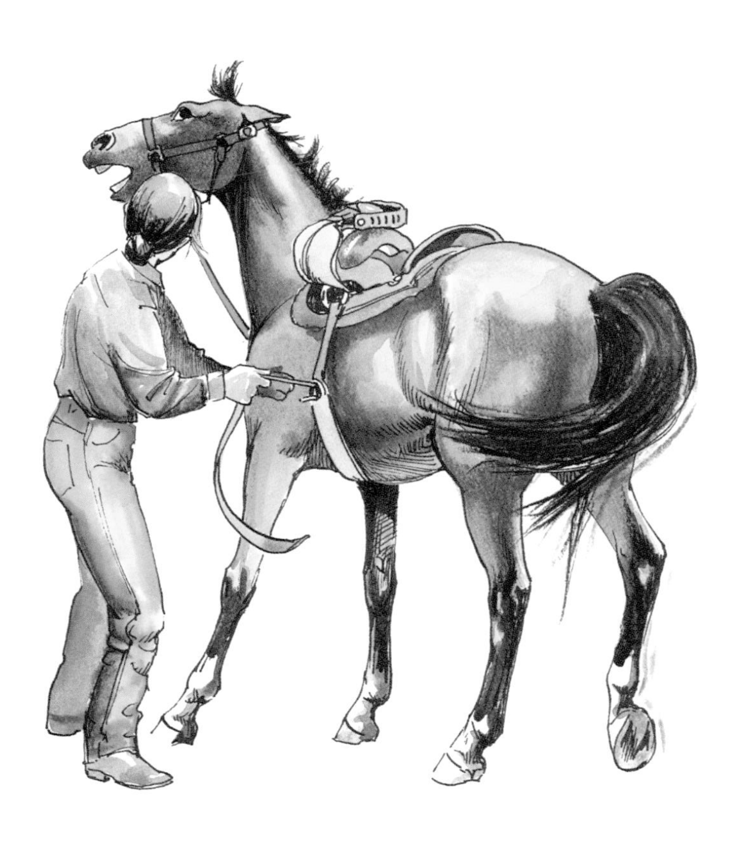

For these horses, you'll need to be extra diligent about watching for the following telltale signs of poor-fitting tack:

Hair loss or raw skin caused by tack that rubs: White spots on some horses' withers are examples of what results from saddles that rub. When the affected area is finally allowed to heal, the hair often grows back white in color as a result of the underlying damage.

Small dry spots on your horse's back, under his saddle blanket: Look for such areas after a ride; they signal that the saddle is digging into your horse's back or pinching at those dry points.

Welts on your horse's body wherever tack comes into contact: Welts indicate inflammation—a sure sign that something doesn't fit correctly.

A "goosey" back: After a ride, run your fingers down both sides of your horse's back simultaneously, placing your fingers approximately two inches away from his spine and using medium pressure. If he flinches or drops his back under the pressure, he's probably back sore, which could be a sign of poor saddle fit.

A saddle that shifts from side to side, even when the cinch or the girth is tight: A properly fitted saddle should stay in place. Your safety, as well as the horse's, is at risk if the saddle slips during a ride.

Horses that are ridden while in pain can become unsound over time. If your horse exhibits any sign of pain, don't make the mistake of thinking he's just overreacting. Replace tack as soon as you detect a problem. Ill-fitting tack will take its toll on

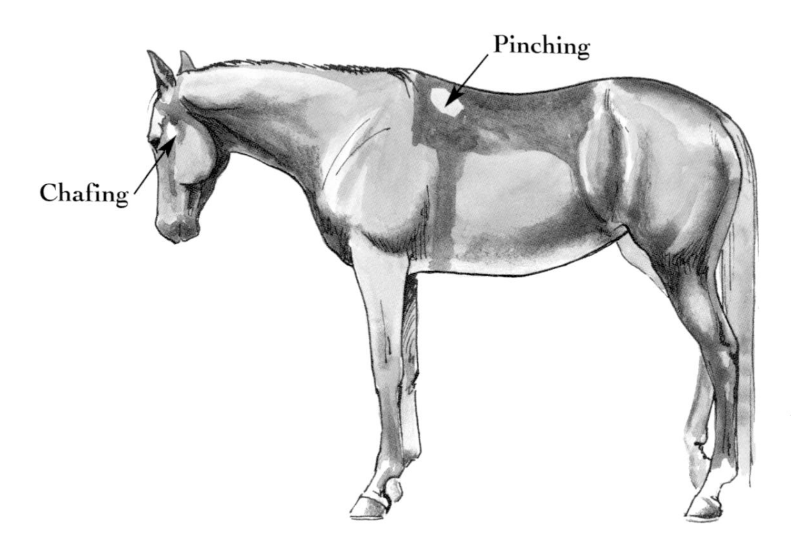

your horse's health and can lead to irreparable damage. It's always better to pay a little extra up front for good-fitting equipment than to pay later on with your horse's well-being.

Sizing Up English and Western Saddles

Saddles come in different styles, shapes, colors, and sizes. Within the English and western riding disciplines, there are different types of saddles to choose from. English saddle types include dressage, jumping, eventing, and saddleseat. Western saddle styles include trail, pleasure, reining, roping, barrel racing, cutting, and working horse. Regardless of the type of saddle you choose, there are basic sizing guidelines to follow when it comes to fit for both you and your horse.

In addition to saddles, girths and cinches have to be correctly sized to ensure proper fit.

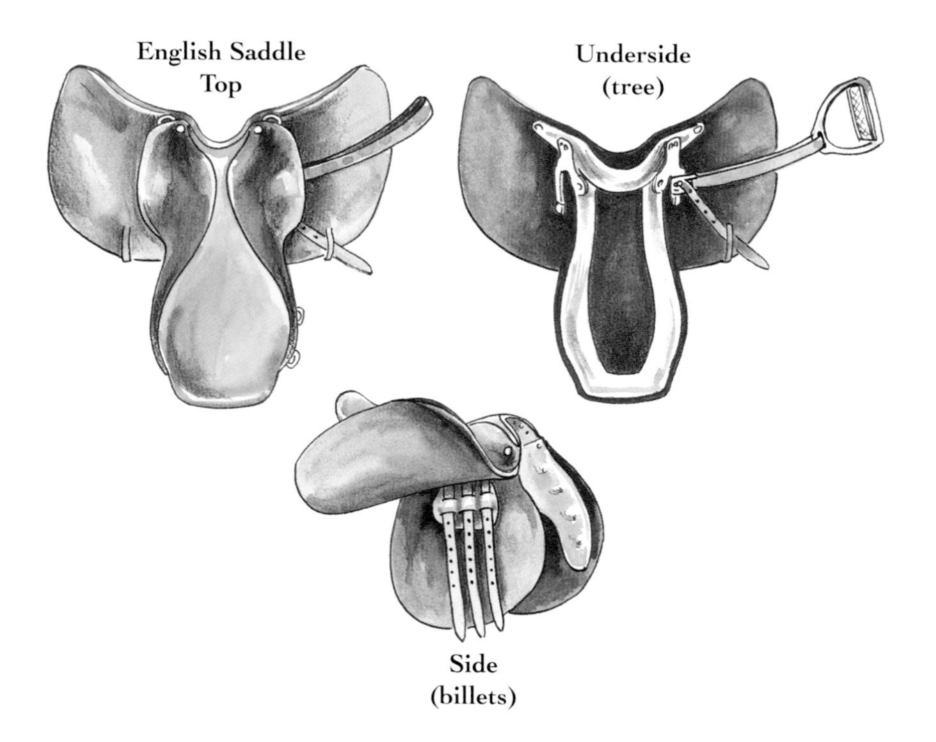
English Saddle
Top
Underside
(tree)
Side
(billets)

Saddle Sizes

Saddles are sized according to their tree sizes and their seat sizes. The tree size determines how the saddle will fit your horse's back. The seat size determines how it will fit your body build.

Tree Sizes

The tree is the foundation on which a saddle is built: it's a saddle's skeleton. It also serves to distribute a rider's weight comfortably over the horse's back. A tree can be made from various materials, including wood, metal, and hard plastic. Some saddles are designed without trees. Treeless saddles have a one-size-fits-all-horses appeal, but they still require some customization by a knowledgeable saddle fitter to ensure a mount's comfort.

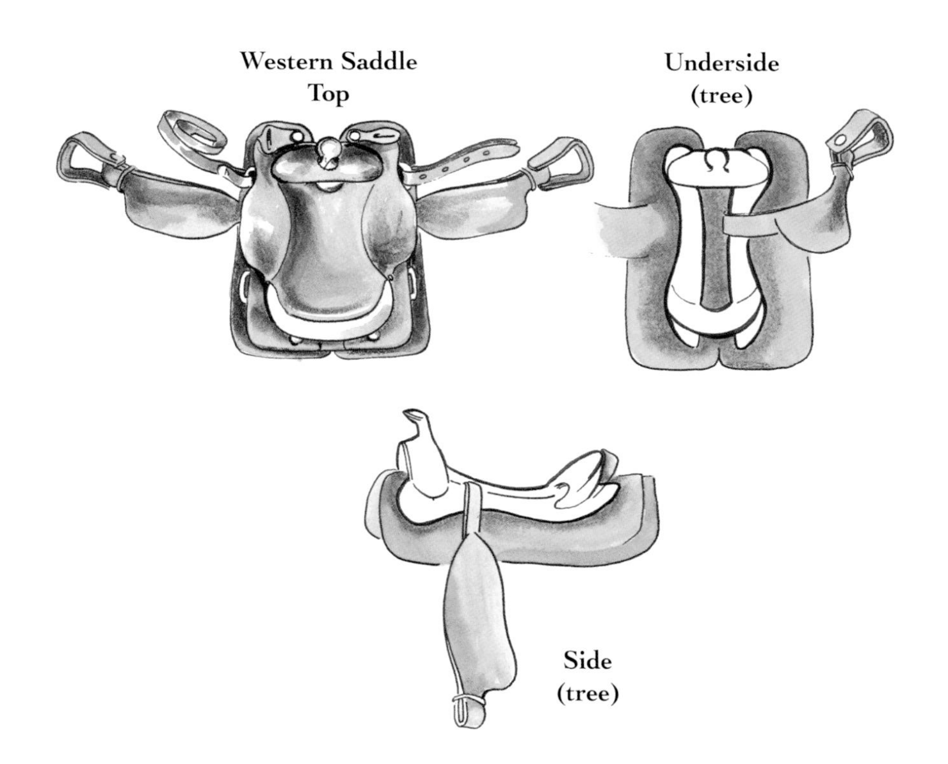
Western Saddle
Top
Underside
(tree)
Side
(tree)

The size of the saddle tree your horse needs is based on her back size and shape. In English saddles, trees are sized as narrow, medium, wide, and extra wide; the sizes correspond to the horse's back width. Western saddle sizes are typically designated as Arab, semi-quarter bar, full-quarter bar, or draft, which correspond to narrow, medium, wide, and extra-wide back sizes.

To measure your horse for her tree size, you'll need a flexicurve (a measuring tool commonly found at art supply stores.) Because a flexicurve is made of pliable plastic or rubber that retains its shape after being bent, it allows you to make a mold of the contour of your horse's back. Flexicurves come in various lengths; one 12 inches long should suffice for measuring your horse, but one 18 inches long would be better.

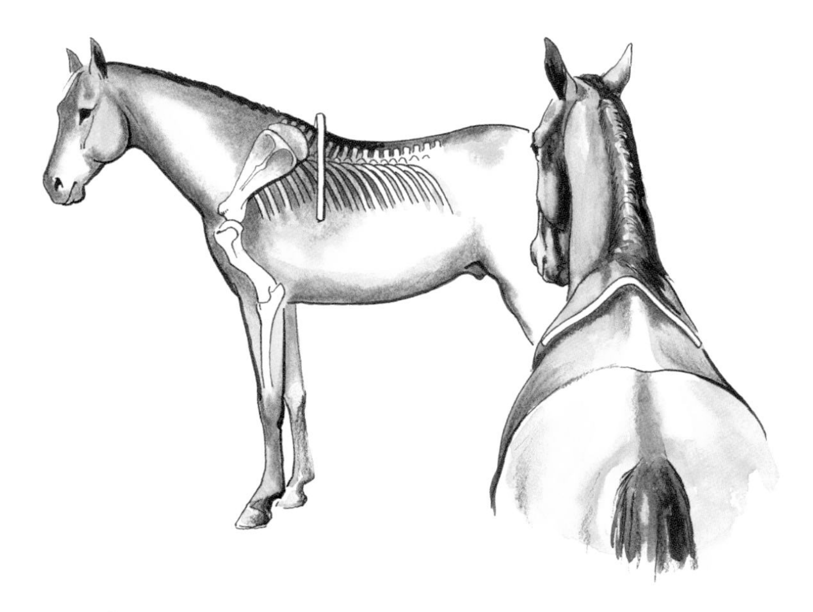

To make a mold of your horse's back, start by standing your horse on level ground. Place the flexicurve about 1½ inches behind her shoulder blades (where the front of the saddle will

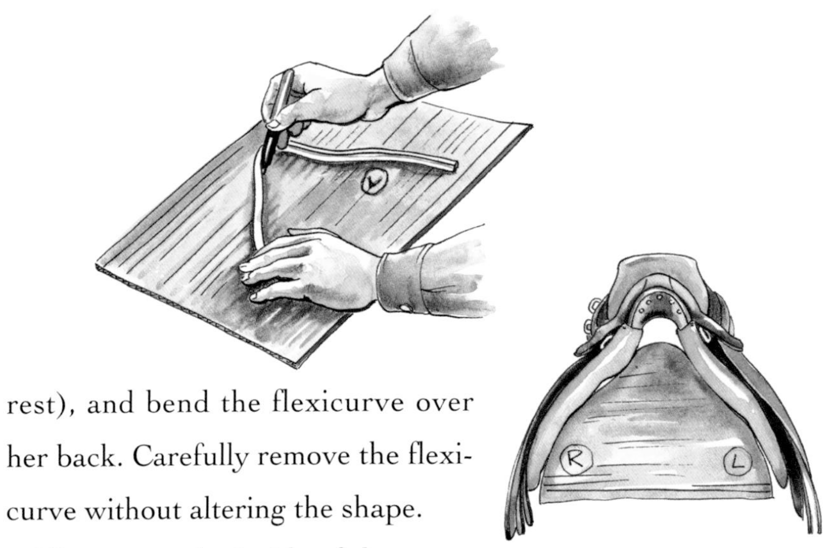

rest), and bend the flexicurve over her back. Carefully remove the flexicurve without altering the shape.

Next, trace the inside of the curve of the flexicurve on a piece of cardboard, and mark the pattern to indicate your horse's right and left sides. Cut the cardboard along your trace marks to create a pattern of the contour of your horse's back. When shopping for saddles, the pattern should fit perfectly under the pommel of the saddle you choose.

Seat Sizes

Seat size is based on rider physique. Riders with long legs or heavy builds usually need a larger saddle seat size; riders who are more petite in stature and build need a smaller seat size.

An English saddle's seat size is calculated by measuring the distance from the screw, or rivet, on the side of the saddle's pommel (the front end) to the top of the cantle (the back end). This measurement generally ranges from 15 to 18 inches, which translates directly to seat sizes 15 to 18.

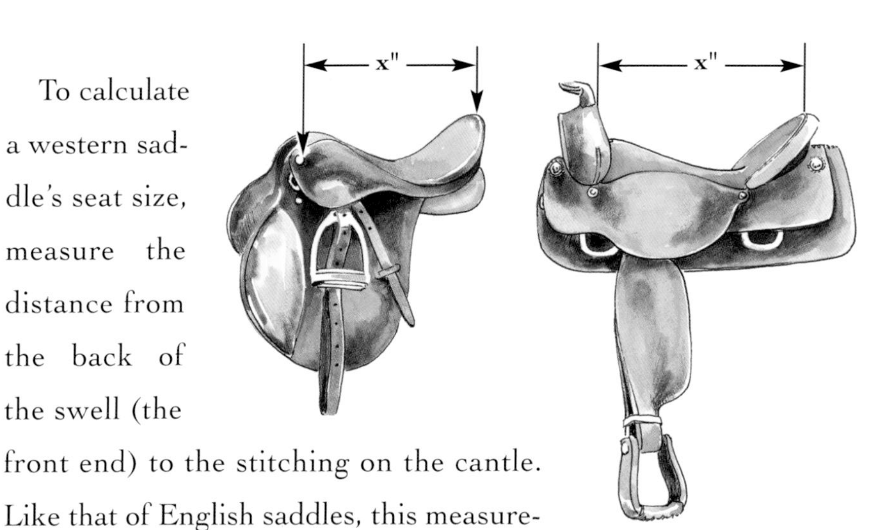

To calculate a western saddle's seat size, measure the distance from the back of the swell (the front end) to the stitching on the cantle. Like that of English saddles, this measurement (in inches) correlates to seat size. (Because English and western saddles are built and measured differently, the sizes don't translate exactly. A size 15 in an English saddle, for example, is not the same as a size 15 in a western saddle.)

The best way to determine which seat size you need is to sit in a variety of saddles of different sizes. When sitting in a saddle, whether it's English or western, you should be able to place a full hand's width both behind and in front of your seat. If you are spilling over or the saddle is too roomy, it's not the right size for you.

A saddle's twist is also a consideration when determining proper seat size. The twist is the narrowest portion of the seat, just behind the pommel, where your legs hang down. Generally, saddles are designed with either a narrow or a wide twist (although any width is possible with a custom saddle maker). If you feel as if you're doing the splits when trying on saddles, chances are you need a narrow twist.

Visually Inspecting the Saddle

Perform a visual inspection of any saddle you are considering buying. In addition to checking tree and seat size, pay attention to a saddle's gullet, the channel on the underside that goes over the horse's spine. The gullet offers clearance, preventing the saddle from pressing directly on the spine. With English saddles, look for one that offers a channel at least three to four fingers wide at the narrowest point. Large horses, such as draft breeds and some warmbloods, may need an even wider gullet channel.

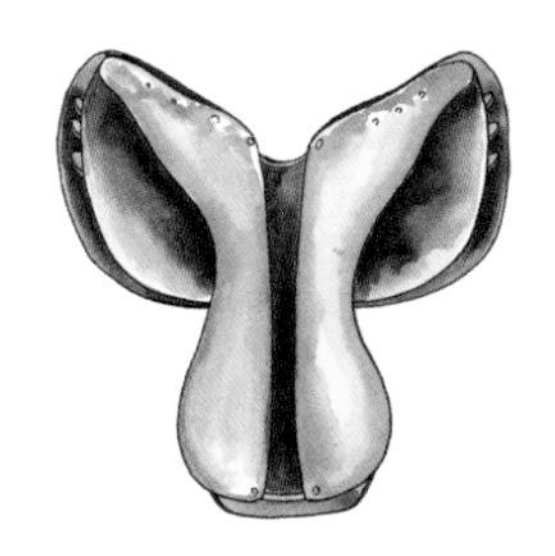

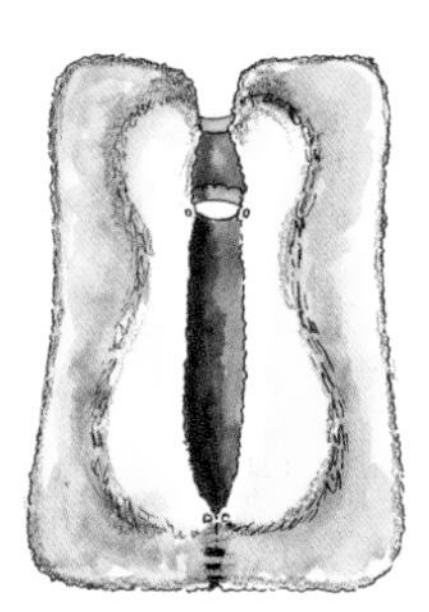

In a western saddle, the gullet is measured across the width of the opening under the pommel. Although the standard gullet width is 6½ to 7 inches for western saddles, use your cardboard pattern as a guide to help determine whether you'll need something larger or smaller.

After checking the gullet, examine the saddle's underside. On English saddles, look at the panels (the padded areas that help distribute rider weight and protect the horse's back during a ride). Panels should be uniform in size (not lopsided), and they shouldn't be too hard. Although western saddles don't have panels, the underside of a western saddle should be uniform as well, and there shouldn't be any lumps or screws protruding through the fleece.

Finally, make sure any saddle you choose is in good repair. Saddles with dry, cracking leather or broken trees are never a good deal, even if they're free! To check for a broken tree, hold the saddle upside down over your leg, and give it a swift twist. There should be little to no give. Do this a few times, twisting in different directions. If there's movement, the tree is probably broken.

Girths and Cinches

Girths and cinches are straps that hold saddles in place on horses' backs. English saddles require girths; western saddles use cinches. Both are made from a myriad of materials, and many offer just a bit of elasticity for the horse's comfort.

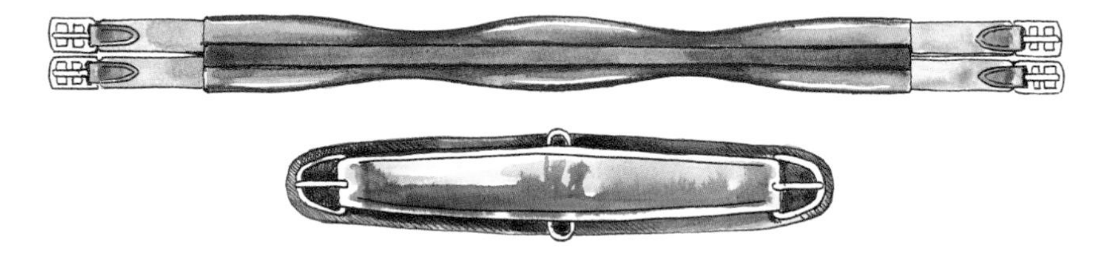

To measure your horse for a girth or a cinch, stand her on a level surface, then correctly position the saddle and pad on her back. For English saddles, use a cloth measuring tape to measure from the middle holes of the saddle's billets (the straps of leather under the saddle flaps that buckle onto the girth) on one side, under the horse's belly, to the middle hole of the saddle's billet on the other side. Keep the measuring tape taut but not tight against her body. The measurement indicated on the tape is the size of the

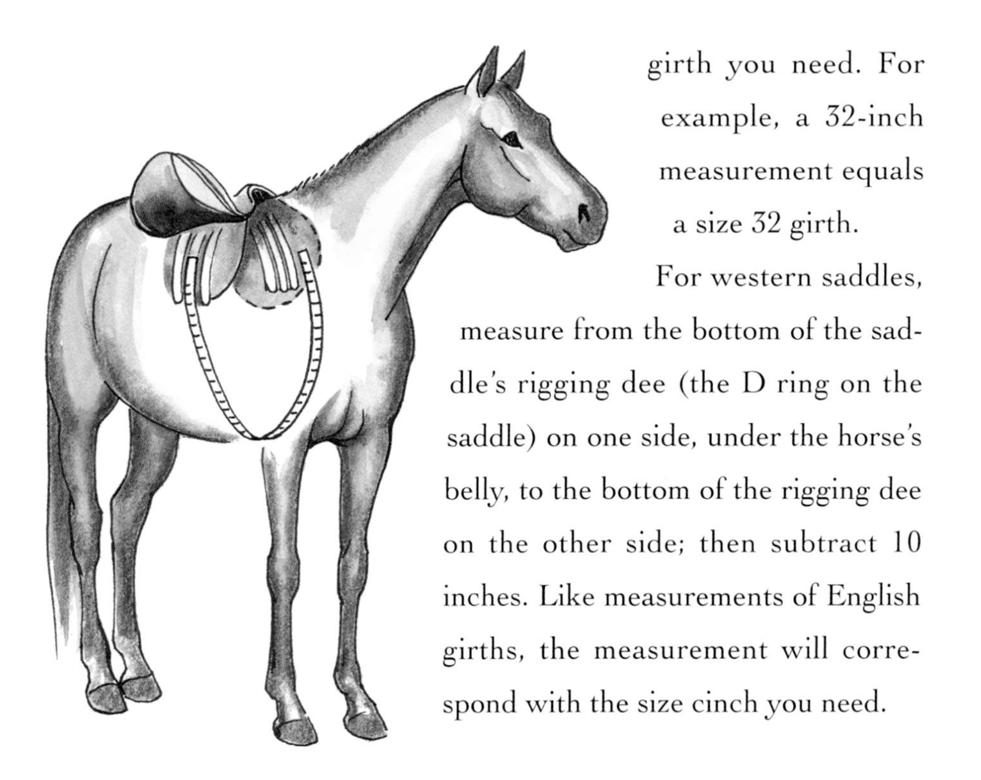

girth you need. For example, a 32-inch measurement equals a size 32 girth.

For western saddles, measure from the bottom of the saddle's rigging dee (the D ring on the saddle) on one side, under the horse's belly, to the bottom of the rigging dee on the other side; then subtract 10 inches. Like measurements of English girths, the measurement will correspond with the size cinch you need.

Make sure you buy a girth or a cinch that is appropriate for your particular saddle type. Different types of saddles, such as dressage and jumping saddles, require different size girths.

Fitting Saddles

Now that you've correctly sized a saddle, it's time to try it on your horse's back. Start by standing your horse on level ground and placing the saddle on his back, without a saddle pad and—if he's quiet—without a girth or a cinch. Place the saddle a bit forward on his back, then gently slip it backward until it won't slip down any farther. Correctly placed, a saddle's seat will rest over the lowest part of the back. At this point, the front edge of the saddle should rest about 1½ inches behind your horse's shoulder blades.

After correctly positioning the saddle on the horse, you will need to inspect for fit while still at the stable, then test the fit on a ride.

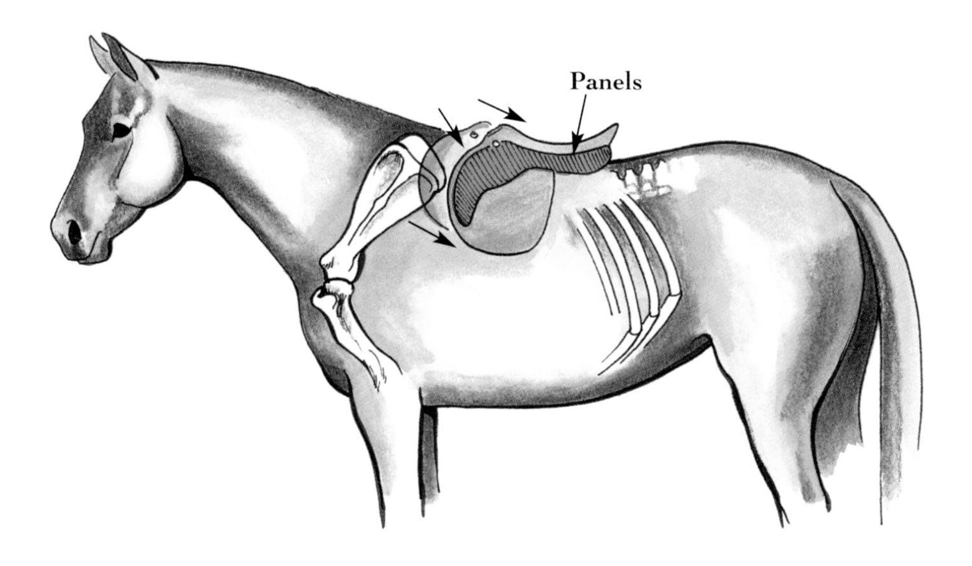

Inspecting the Fit

To inspect the saddle's fit, walk around your horse, and check to make sure the saddle looks balanced and straight over his back.

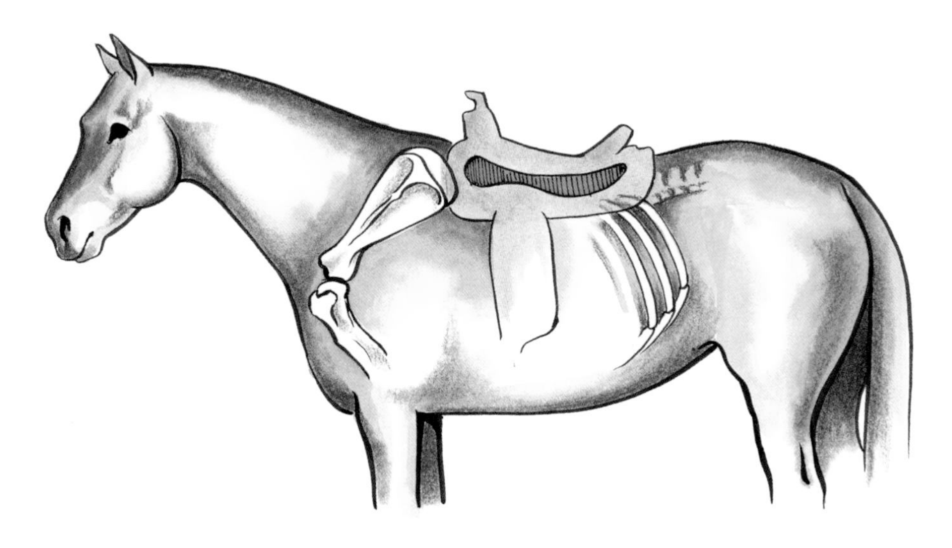

Using the palm of your hand, feel under the saddle to ensure it lies smoothly against the back—there shouldn't be any gaps, or bridging, anywhere. Place your palm under the pommel, and move it along your horse's shoulders, paying particular attention to any areas that seem tight. Tight spots are pressure points that pinch your horse once the girth or the cinch is tightened and rider weight is added. If you feel them, the saddle is too small. If the saddle sloshes from side to side, however, it's probably too big.

Additionally, look at your horse's withers. Is the saddle clearing the withers by about three fingers' width? Less clearance than that indicates the tree size is too large; more clearance indicates the tree size is too small. If your horse has very high withers, you can buy an English saddle that is cut back over the withers to eliminate rubbing; if you ride in a western saddle, ask for a saddle with high pommel clearance.

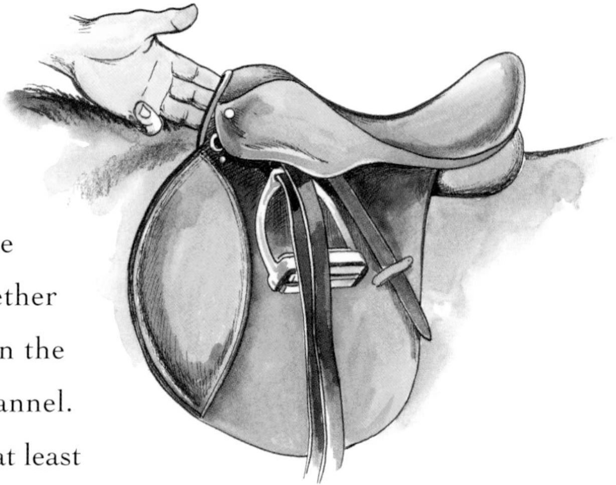

To inspect the fit of an English saddle, stand behind your horse and check whether you can see down the entire gullet channel. There should be at least an inch of clearance between his spine and the saddle. The saddle shouldn't come into contact with your horse's lumbar region either. Make sure the cantle doesn't extend past your horse's last rib, using your hand to feel for his ribs.

Next, try adding a pad under the saddle. Pads are designed to help keep saddles clean and in place as well as to offer protection for horses' backs. New styles designed for equine sore backs and poor-fitting saddles abound, but a well-fitting saddle should not require special pads. And piling on excess padding is not going to make the saddle fit better. A standard fleece pad for English saddles and a 1-inch-thick wool pad for western saddles should suffice. The pad you choose should be clean and free of burrs and other foreign material. When your horse is tacked up, the pad should extend past the saddle by an inch or so (English) to 3 to 4 inches (western).

The next step when inspecting a saddle's fit is to attach the girth or the cinch, tightening it in stages. When you're done, you

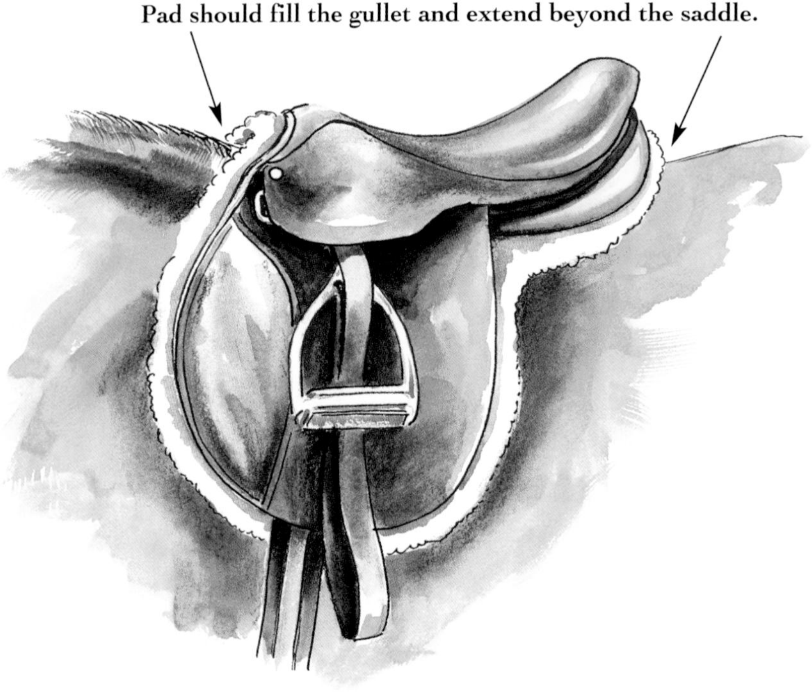

Pad should fill the gullet and extend beyond the saddle.

should be able to slide your fingers (in a flat position) between the girth or the cinch and your horse's belly. More slack than that, however, and the saddle will slip out of position.

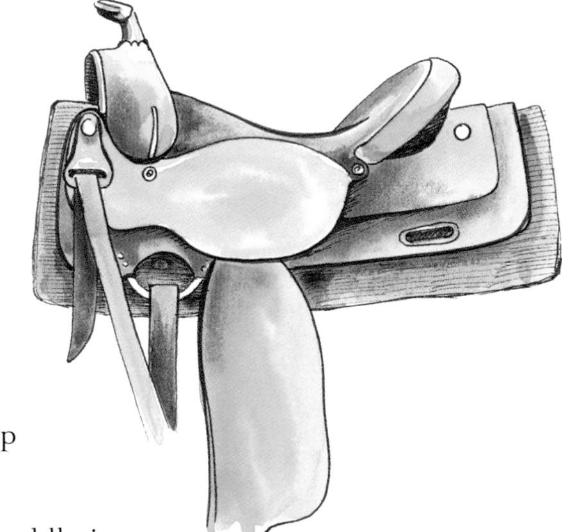

If your western saddle is designed to accommodate a rear cinch, tighten it enough to prevent your horse's hind legs from getting caught, but don't tighten it as much as the front cinch. You should be able to slide your fist between the rear cinch and your horse's belly.

Testing the Fit

If the fit of the saddle passes your scrutiny, take your horse for a spin, and work him at all gaits. He should be moving freely forward without hesitation. After you remove the saddle, look for any small dry patches on your horse's coat. If he worked up a light sweat, his back should be uniformly wet in the area directly under the saddle; small dry patches are a good indication of pinching.

If you continually ride in a saddle that pinches, your horse will develop sores or white hairs under these pressure points, signaling

serious long-term health problems to come. In some cases, an experienced saddle fitter may be able to adjust the saddle, but more than likely it will need to be replaced.

Fitting Bridles, Reins, and Bits

Bridles, reins, and bits come in many different styles for both English and western riders. The styles you choose are based on fit, the type of riding you do, your horse's training level, and your riding skills.

Bridles

English bridles typically come in the following sizes: pony, cob, full, and warmblood or oversize. The most common styles are dressage and hunter-jumper designs. These styles differ, but the fit rules are basically the same.

Western bridles differ from their English counterparts in that they are often designed to be used without a cavesson (noseband). Western bridles come in many different styles—with or without a browbrand, and one or double ear—but all are typically available in three sizes: pony, Arabian, and horse. Pony and Arabian sizes are for smaller horses; the horse size is designed to fit the average stock horse, such as the American Quarter Horse,

the American Paint Horse, and the Appaloosa. Unfortunately, if you happen to own a large horse, say a draft breed or a warmblood type, you won't have much luck finding a true western bridle to fit her. You'll need to either find a custom bridle or opt for an English style.

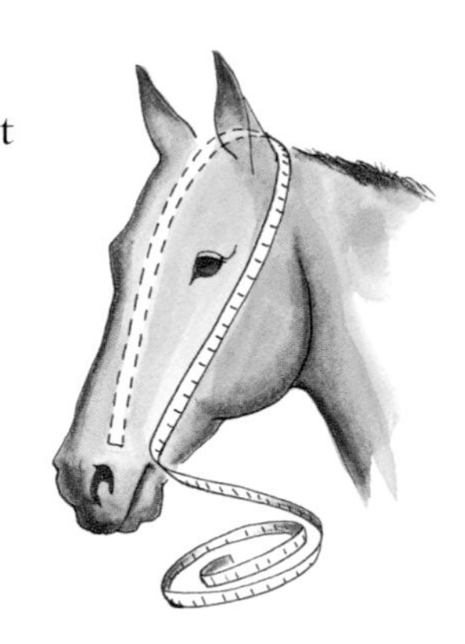

To fit an English or a western bridle, start by measuring your horse's headstall size. The headstall is the part of the bridle that goes over the horse's head, just behind her ears. Using a cloth tape measure, measure from one corner of her mouth, around her poll (the area just behind the horse's ears), to the corner of her mouth on the other side. When sizing your horse for a noseband, measure the circumference of her face just below the cheekbone and curve of the jaw. Take these measurements, along with your tape measure, to your local tack store. Determine your horse's bridle size using the standard size designations (pony, full, and so on). When you find a bridle, compare its measurements (using your tape measure) with those of your horse.

When trying a bridle on your horse, use the following techniques to ensure a comfortable fit. Allow a finger's width clearance between the fastened cavesson and the horse's nose. You should also be able to fit your fist between your horse's jawline and the buckled throatlatch (the piece that attaches under the throat). Additionally, look for any bridle components that may rub or cause irritation. Pay particular attention to the browband; it should sit well above your horse's eyes but far enough below her ears that it doesn't rub. If sores or white hairs develop under the bridle after use, return it or have an expert review your tack to ensure it's properly adjusted.

Reins

English bridles are usually sold with reins, but expect to buy reins separately for a western bridle. Regardless of the bridle style and type of riding you do, the length of reins you choose should be long enough to allow your horse to stretch his neck toward the ground without your having to lean forward when in the saddle.

Standard English rein length is 54 inches, but some companies offer a 60-inch length to accommodate large horses. Western split reins, a common style that doesn't have a buckle to keep the reins together, are typically available in 84-inch lengths. The extra length is needed to cross over the horse's withers so the rider doesn't lose the reins.

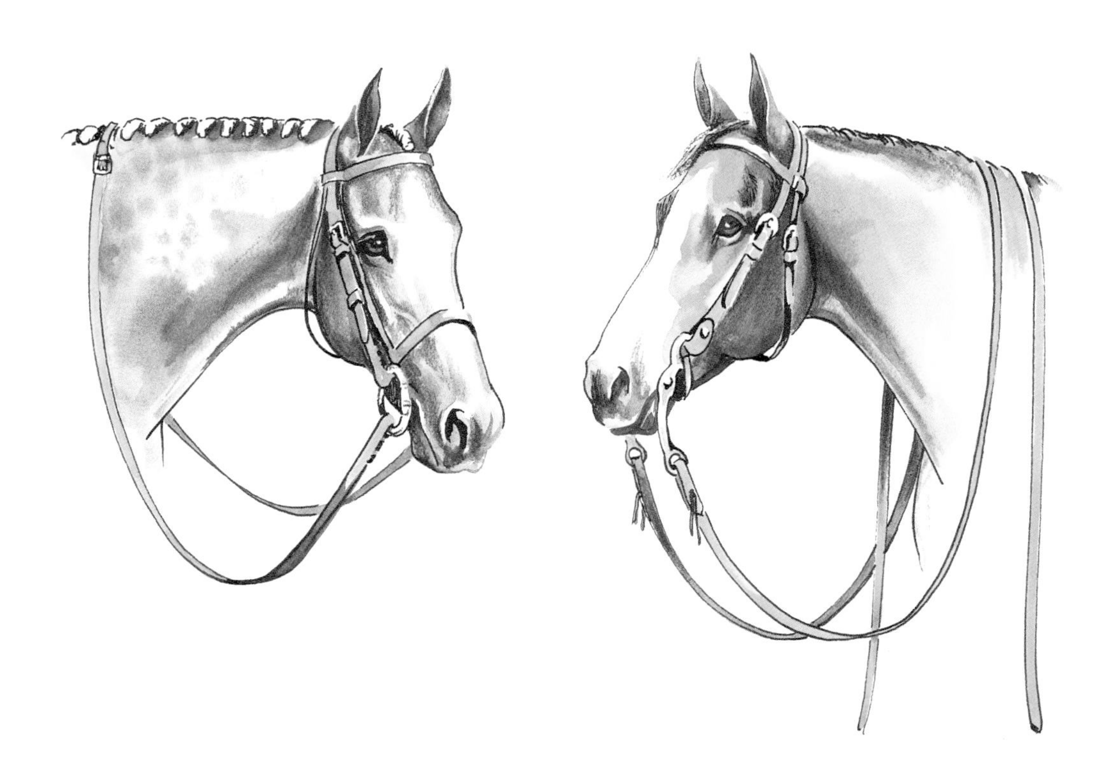

Bits

Once you have your bridle and reins, you'll probably need a bit to make your horse's headgear complete. Bits come in two basic designs: direct contact and leverage. Commonly used direct contact bits include snaffle designs. Because snaffle bits are simple, they are often used in the English disciplines and on young western horses. Most western trainers start their beginning western riders on horses tacked up in snaffle bits. Leverage-type curb bits have shanks that provide leverage. Curb bits are used on well-trained western horses as well as on upper-level dressage horses.

The type of bit you use depends on your riding skills and your horse's training level. Always opt for a bit that keeps your horse

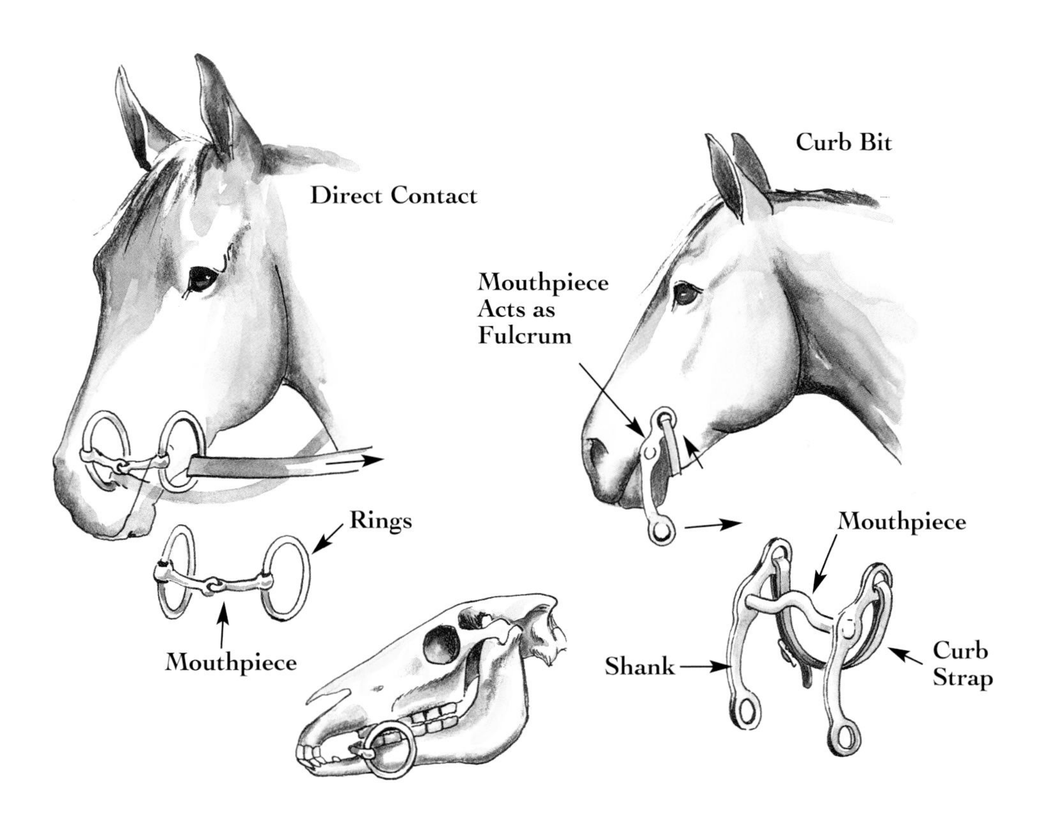
Direct Contact
Rings
Mouthpiece
Curb Bit
Mouthpiece
Acts as
Fulcrum
Mouthpiece
Shank
Curb
Strap

comfortable. A jointed snaffle, with its smooth finish and medium thickness, is a good starting bit.

To ensure correct bit size, you'll need to measure your horse's mouth to learn how wide her mouthpiece needs to be. Using a piece of string, measure her mouth as follows: place the string where

the bit would lie in her mouth, measure her mouth from corner to corner, and then add ½ inch. The extra length prevents pinching at the corners of the horse's mouth. Bits are sized in ¼-inch increments (4¾ inch, 5 inch, and so on). Although the most common bit size is 5 inches, your horse may need a smaller or larger bit.

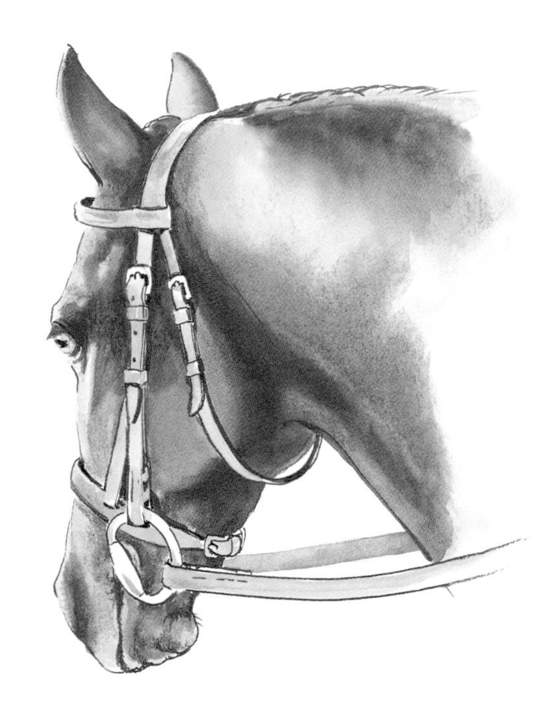

When bridling up your horse with any bit, use caution and start off conservatively so the bit doesn't pinch the mouth. First, adjust the sides of the bridle so the bit causes a single wrinkle at each corner of her mouth. For horses outfitted in a snaffle bit, two wrinkles may be warranted for proper fit. Keep in mind, however, that these are merely guidelines, not hard-and-fast rules. Because every horse is different, finding the best bit position in the horse's mouth takes some experimentation.

If you are using a curb bit, the curb chain or strap is correctly adjusted when you can place a finger under it and the shanks of the curb are at a 45-degree angle to the line of the horse's mouth when the reins are used. Curb hooks should face forward: the hook opening should face the direction the horse is facing.

Bitless Bridles

Some bridles are meant to be used bitless, as some horses are more responsive or more comfortable without a bit in their mouths. Sidepulls and hackamores, for example, are two bitless options.

The reins on sidepulls attach to either side of the noseband. Sidepulls are usually considered less severe than hackamores, but they don't offer a great deal of control.

Most sidepulls are fitted to your horse the same way bitted bridles are; hackamores are slightly different.

There are generally two types of hackamores: traditional and mechanical. Traditional hackamores used for western riding, often referred to as bosals, use headstalls, as do other western

bridles. However, unlike a regular cavesson, the noseband on a traditional hackamore floats above the horse's face. With mechanical hackamores, available in western and English styles, the noseband actually touches the horse's face, and the reins are attached to metal shanks.

Tacking Up Your Horse's Legs

There are many products available to help protect your horse's lower legs and hooves from injury while he exercises. Although these products can't prevent all injuries, they help protect against interference injuries caused by opposing legs and hooves. Certain leg-protection products also help shield and support tendons and ligaments during exercise, which may stave off some soft-tissue injuries.

When it comes to fitting and applying protective legwear for your horse, different guidelines apply, depending on the tack you use. The following are some of the most common types of leg protection for your horse.

Polo wraps: These one-size-fits-all, bandagelike fabric wraps feature Velcro closures. When applying, use steady, even pressure, and wrap toward the back. Wrapping too tightly can lead to tendon and ligament injury; a loose, sloppy wrap can slip out of place. When finished wrapping, you should be able to fit a finger inside each wrap.

Sport, splint, and jumping boots: These boots also protect the lower legs but are a little easier to work with than polo wraps are. Neoprene and leather are the most commonly used boot materials; Velcro or buckle closures keep the boots securely in place. Manufacturers size their boots to help eliminate the fit guesswork. Sizing is based on the length and circumference of your horse's legs. Follow the manufacturer directions when fitting and applying these boot types, as every brand is unique. Most manufacturers also mark their boots for left front leg, right front leg, and so on.

These boots should fit snugly enough to stay in place during exercise but not so tightly that they cause injury to your horse. As a general rule, you should be able to comfortably slip a finger

inside each boot when your horse is outfitted; if the boot shifts once it's on, it's too big.

Bell boots: Made of neoprene, rubber, or heavy canvas, bell boots cover only the horse's hooves. Bell boots are most commonly used on front hooves to protect against overreaching, that is, when a hind hoof strikes the heel bulbs on a front hoof. Bell boots come in extra-small, small, medium, large, and extra-large sizes. A horse's hoof and leg size dictate the bell boot size he'll need. Be aware, however, that there isn't always a correlation between leg and hoof size. Some tall horses have small hooves and bones, whereas some short horses are well endowed in these areas!

Bell boots should not rub anywhere on your horse's legs or heel bulbs; you should be able to comfortably fit a finger's

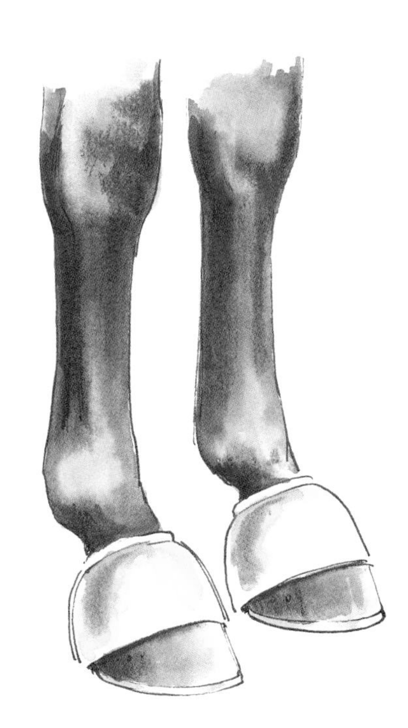

width between the top of the boot and your horse's leg. The boots should be long enough to cover your horse's heel bulbs but not so long that he'll step on the boots.

Whatever legwear you choose for your horse, be sure to examine his legs after he exercises in them. If there are any signs of swelling, blistering, hair loss, or excess heat, stop using the product and call your veterinarian. Some horses are allergic to materials commonly used to make boots, and some horses simply can't tolerate the excess heat generated by certain legwear designs.

The rewards of well-fitting tack are great. Your horse will behave better, be a more willing partner, and be at less risk for injury. As a result, you'll both have happy trails ahead.

About the Author

Toni McAllister is the managing editor for *Horse Illustrated* magazine, an award-winning publication that targets equestrians of all disciplines and skill levels. She has written several articles about horses and finds particular enjoyment in covering equine health-care topics. Based in Southern California, McAllister is a horse owner who currently enjoys dressage as well as trail riding. She spent several years riding hunt seat and has dabbled in various western riding disciplines.